BLOODLINES

DEADLY CONFLICT BETWEEN THE HATFIELDS AND McCOYS

Bloodlines: Deadly Conflict Between the Hatfields and McCoys

Whitman
Publishing, LLC
PUBLISHING SINCE 1934
www.whitman.com
© 2012 Whitman Publishing, LLC

ISBN: 0794838022
Printed and assembled in the United States of America.

To view other products from Whitman Publishing, please visit Whitman.com.

Scan the QR code above to browse
Whitman Publishing's full selection
of specialty books.

INTRODUCTION

America's most notorious family feud was officially put to rest over 120 years ago. However, the names of the Hatfield and McCoy families are today still synonymous with obsession, violence and an all-consuming desire for revenge.

It all started in 1865 with the murder of unionist Asa McCoy, brother of McCoy patriarch Randolph "Randall" McCoy, by the confederate uncle of Hatfield clan leader William "Devil Anse" Hatfield. The ill feelings between the families seethed beneath the surface until the day in 1878 when Randall accused Devil Anse's cousin Floyd of stealing one of his prized hogs. The ensuing trial — presided over by a Hatfield judge — triggered a firestorm of brutality and vigilantism that would engulf the sleepy Tug Fork Valley and catapult the feuding clans into the spotlight of the national media.

In the world of 19th century "yellow journalism," the feud had all the elements of a terrific, surreal story. In true Romeo-and-Juliet fashion, McCoy's daughter ran off with Hatfield's son, only to be jilted and abandoned later. Three of McCoy's sons killed Devil Anse's younger brother during a drunken election-day brawl. This led to the gruesome vigilante-style execution of the McCoy boys by a Hatfield posse. Later, the McCoy home was attacked by a group of vengeful Hatfields, rumored to have been led by Devil Anse himself. The cabin was burned to the ground, Randall's son and 13-year-old daughter were killed, and his wife Sarah was left for dead after being savagely beaten. The sensational trial that followed — which sent seven Hatfields to prison and one to the gallows — shocked many Americans.

The deadly Hatfield-McCoy conflict officially ended with the trial's conclusion in 1891, but the legend of the feuding mountain clans continues to hold the public's imagination over a century later. The events that occurred on the West Virginia-Kentucky border have never vanished into history, instead kept alive by dozens of books, documentaries and films. The now-mythic tale, and the characters surrounding it, endures — timeless, fresh and alive. We continue to remain just as shocked and fascinated by the Hatfield-McCoy feud as the public was over 120 years ago.

— *Christopher Marsden*

HATFIELD FAMILY TREE

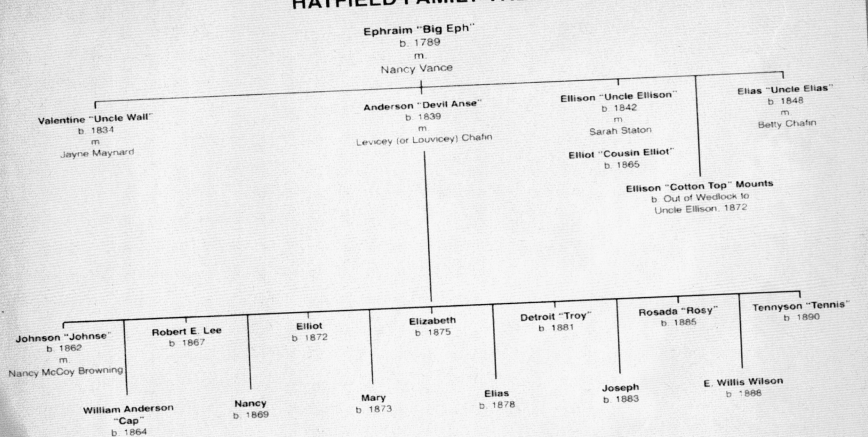

Ephraim "Big Eph"
b. 1789
m.
Nancy Vance

Valentine "Uncle Wall"
b. 1834
m.
Jayne Maynard

Anderson "Devil Anse"
b. 1839
m.
Levicey (or Louvicey) Chafin

Ellison "Uncle Ellison"
b. 1842
m.
Sarah Staton

Elliot "Cousin Elliot"
b. 1865

Elias "Uncle Elias"
b. 1848
m.
Betty Chafin

Ellison "Cotton Top" Mounts
b. Out of Wedlock to
Uncle Ellison, 1872

Johnson "Johnse"
b. 1862
m.
Nancy McCoy Browning

William Anderson "Cap"
b. 1864

Robert E. Lee
b. 1867

Nancy
b. 1869

Elliot
b. 1872

Mary
b. 1873

Elizabeth
b. 1875

Elias
b. 1878

Detroit "Troy"
b. 1881

Joseph
b. 1883

Rosada "Rosy"
b. 1885

E. Willis Wilson
b. 1888

Tennyson "Tennis"
b. 1890

HATFIELD

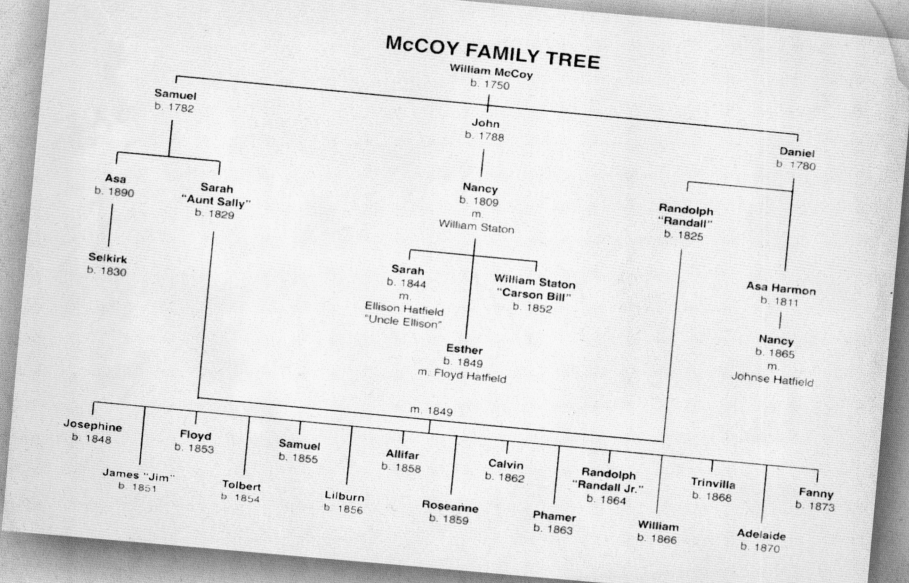

McCOY FAMILY TREE

William McCoy
b. 1750

Samuel
b. 1782

John
b. 1788

Daniel
b. 1780

Asa
b. 1890

Sarah "Aunt Sally"
b. 1829

Nancy
b. 1809
m.
William Staton

Randolph "Randall"
b. 1825

Selkirk
b. 1830

Sarah
b. 1844
m.
Ellison Hatfield
"Uncle Ellison"

William Staton "Carson Bill"
b. 1852

Asa Harmon
b. 1811

Esther
b. 1849
m. Floyd Hatfield

Nancy
b. 1865
m.
Johnse Hatfield

m. 1849

Josephine
b. 1848

James "Jim"
b. 1851

Floyd
b. 1853

Tolbert
b. 1854

Samuel
b. 1855

Lilburn
b. 1856

Allifar
b. 1858

Roseanne
b. 1859

Calvin
b. 1862

Phamer
b. 1863

Randolph "Randall Jr."
b. 1864

William
b. 1866

Trinvilla
b. 1868

Adelaide
b. 1870

Fanny
b. 1873

Arguably one of the best-known photographs associated with the famous Hatfield-McCoy feud, this 1897 image depicts William Anderson "Devil Anse" Hatfield sitting with his extended family. To the extreme right stands W.S. Borden, a local merchant who commissioned the picture. Also pictured are: (back row, left to right) Rosada or Rose Lee, daughter; Detroit (Troy), son; Betty Hatfield Caldwell, daughter; Elias Hatfield, son; Tom Chafin, nephew; Joe Hatfield, son; Ock Damron, a hired hand; Shephard Hatfield, son of Cap; Coleman, son of Cap; Levicy Emma, daughter of Cap; Bill Borden, local merchant; (middle row) Mary Hensley-Simkins-Howe, daughter of Devil Anse, with her child Vici Simkins; William "Devil Anse" Hatfield; Levicy Hatfield, wife of Devil Anse; Nancy Elizabeth, wife of Cap, with her child Robert Elliot on lap; Louise, daughter of Cap; Cap Hatfield, holding rifle; (front row) Tennyson (Tennis), son of Devil Anse; Vicy, daughter of Johnse Hatfield; Willis, son of Devil Anse; and Yellow Watch, Devil Anse's hunting dog.

Dameron, Elias Hatfield, Troy Hatfield, Rose Hatfield, Joe Hatfield
ap Hatfield   Anse Hatfield Lauricy Hatfield

A few minutes after the preceding photo was taken, Borden rearranged his subjects and had the photographer shoot this image. Here we see (left to right) the Hatfield's hired man, Ock Damron, and sons Elias, Detroit (Troy), Joe and Cap. William Borden stands at far right. Seated in front are Tennis, Devil Anse and Willis Hatfield. Barely visible behind the men are Levicy Hatfield and daughter Mary.

This rifle, now in the collection of the Kentucky Historical Society, once belonged to Devil Anse Hatfield.

Born in 1825, Randolph "Randall" McCoy grew up in the Tug River Valley, which marked the boundary between Kentucky and West Virginia. One of 13 children, he was born on the Kentucky side of the valley. There he learned hunting and farming techniques necessary for survival in the Appalachian Mountains. McCoy was no stranger to hardship during his early years. His father, Daniel, was often away, and his mother, Margaret, struggled to provide for her large family.

In 1849, McCoy married his first cousin, Sarah "Sally" McCoy. A few years later, his wife inherited land from her father, and the couple settled on a 300-acre spread in Pike County, Kentucky, where they began to raise 16 children.

During the Civil War, McCoy served in the Confederacy, perhaps in the same local militia as Devil Anse Hatfield. After a brief skirmish, he was captured by Union troops in 1863, and spent the next two years in a prisoner-of-war camp in Ohio.

William Anderson "Devil Anse" Hatfield was born in 1839, one of 18 children born to Ephraim and Nancy Hatfield, and raised in Logan County, West Virginia, in the Tug River Valley. Known throughout the valley for being an excellent shot and horseman, the locals claimed he earned his nickname due to the fact he was so powerful and intimidating that he could take on the devil himself. In 1861, Hatfield married the daughter of a neighboring farmer, Levicy Chafin. Soon after the marriage he quickly joined the Confederate cause during the Civil War, heading up a local militia known as the Logan Wildcats with his equally fierce uncle Jim Vance.

Devil Anse Hatfield

When the War Between the States came to its bloody conclusion, Devil Anse Hatfield and the Logan Wildcats militia continued to wreak havoc among all of the citizens of Logan County whom they suspected of having Union ties and sympathies.

Like many Southerners, Devil Anse returned home to find his homestead in great disrepair and his family nearly starving. This only fueled his hatred of the Northerners and his desire to seek revenge.

Unlike his brother Randall, Asa Harmon McCoy had definite Union sympathies. He joined the Union cause early on in the war, but was discharged in 1862 after suffering a broken leg. He returned home to recover, but many historians suspect he may have been employed as a Union spy. In 1864 he received a warning from Jim Vance, uncle of Devil Anse Hatfield, that he could soon expect a "visit" from the dreaded Logan Wildcats.

A few days after the warning from Jim Vance, alarmed by the sound of nearby gunfire, Asa Harmon McCoy left his property and hid in a nearby cave that was stocked with food and water by his slave, Pete. Following Pete's tracks in the snow, the Logan Wildcats learned the location of Asa Harmon's hideout and he was killed during a barrage of gunshots on Jan. 7, 1865.

DID YOU KNOW?

After the passing of nearly 150 years, it is unlikely we will ever know who actually fired the fatal shot that killed Asa Harmon McCoy. It is almost certain, however, that members of the Hatfield clan were present. In an ironic twist of fate, some members of the McCoy family believed that Asa deserved what he got after betraying his Southern heritage when he sided with the Yankees. The case was never tried, and no one was ever arrested for the killing.

As suggested in this period photo, many men returning to their Southern homes after the war were ragged, bitter and disillusioned. This feeling may well have led to the murder of known Union sympathizer Asa Harmon McCoy. At first, authorities considered Logan Wildcat leader Devil Anse Hatfield to be the prime suspect. However, an iron-clad alibi – he was confirmed to have been confined to his bed – quickly diverted the suspicion to Jim Vance. Eventually, the case went nowhere, and a suspect was never brought to trial.

SITE OF KILLING OF
ASA HARMON McCOY

Asa Harmon McCoy, a Union soldier, was shot in 1865 by the Logan Wildcats. The Wildcats were led by Confederate "Devil Anse" Hatfield. Jim Vance was the suspected leader in the murder, although there was never a conviction. This was the first incident between the two families.
Presented by Pikeville - Pike County Tourism

This historic marker denotes the place where Asa Harmon McCoy was killed by the Logan Wildcats in January 1865. To many, this event was a precursor to the events that would lead up to the great Hatfield-McCoy feud.

In 1877, 12 years after the end of the war, Devil Anse Hatfield was becoming a man of property and influence in Logan County. Many claimed this was due to the fact that his extensive clan had begun to infiltrate local law enforcement and government offices.

DID YOU KNOW?

Many Hatfields served in West Virginia political offices over the years, beginning with Judge "Preacher" Anderson Hatfield — cousin of Devil Anse — who presided over the Hog Trial. As the decades wore on, other Hatfield men served as local administrators, mayors and county sheriffs.

That same year, Devil Anse became embroiled in a land dispute with Randall McCoy's cousin, Perry Cline. In most Appalachian communities, land (such as the swath of Pike County land seen here) was equated with wealth and prestige. Devil Anse emerged victorious and was granted Cline's entire 5,000-acre property. The McCoys, increasingly bitter, felt that old Devil Anse had once again used his political and familial connections to influence the court's decision against the much poorer and less influential McCoy family.

In the fall of 1878, Randolph McCoy learned that one of his best hogs had been stolen from his property. He immediately brought charges against Floyd Hatfield (left) for committing the crime. The ensuing trial was presided over by "Preacher" Anderson Hatfield, Devil Anse's cousin. The star witness was Bill Staton, Randolph McCoy's nephew. He also happened to be the brother-in-law of Devil Anse. Staton swore under oath that the pig in question belonged to Floyd Hatfield.

DID YOU KNOW?

Throughout the 19th century, many cash-strapped folks traded for goods using the barter system, and especially valuable were hogs. In many mountain communities, land boundaries could be vague, and livestock roamed relatively free, but ownership was identified by notches cut into the animals' ears. Randall accused Devil Anse's cousin Floyd of altering those notches so the hog would appear to be his.

When the jury reached its verdict, Selkirk McCoy, nephew of Sarah McCoy, sided with the Hatfields in favor of Floyd. Compared to the McCoys, the Hatfields had some standing in the community. Devil Anse's burgeoning lumber business provided well for his family, but he also employed McCoy family members, including Selkirk.

KIRK McCOY

Many locals were familiar with the fact that at one time, Randall had somehow slighted Selkirk McCoy, who decided to throw in his vote with the Hatfield side of jury, thus allowing Floyd to keep the pig. The McCoy clan would turn their anger not against Selkirk but on star witness Bill Stanton, who was later murdered by Randall's sons Paris and Sam for Stanton's damning testimony. The McCoy boys were acquitted of the crime the following year.

HOG TRIAL

In 1873 Randolph McCoy accused Floyd Hatfield of stealing his hog. A trial followed, presided over by Reverend Anderson Hatfield, justice of the peace. To be fair, the jury consisted of six Hatfields and six McCoys. One witness, William Staton, stated he had seen Floyd mark the hog's ear. This resulted in Floyd's acquittal.

Presented by Pikeville-Pike County Tourism

2001   KENTUCKY HISTORICAL SOCIETY   KENTUCKY DEPARTMENT OF HIGHWAYS   2005

This marker denotes the location of the infamous "Hog Trial" that most historians agree marked the beginning of the bloody Hatfield-McCoy feud.

Throughout the 1890s and 1900s, Devil Anse Hatfield and his relatives appeared all too eager to pose for photographs taken by members of the media who were interested in reporting on the sensational and increasingly gory case. Many members of the family lived to regret this cooperation.

DID YOU KNOW?

Gun ownership in the Tug River Valley was not only commonplace but it was necessary for survival. During the early years of the feud, both families probably used early 19th century longrifles owned by their ancestors, in addition to Civil War bring-backs. Photos taken in the late 1890s show that the Hatfields eventually upgraded their weaponry to include a Winchester Model 1873 and a Model 1892. A 7.5-inch-barreled Colt Single-Action Army revolver and several Smith & Wesson New Model Frontier revolvers also became part of the arsenal.

Many of the photos taken by the media during, and immediately after, the 1889 Hatfield trial were carefully composed to portray the Hatfields as violent, backward "hillbillies." Due in large part to these stereotyped images, the country harshly judged the people of West Virginia and Kentucky for decades to come.

Devil Anse Hatfield (first on left) and various armed and unidentified members of his family pose circa 1890 in front of what may be the cabin of his son Elias.

Dressed in their Sunday best, the Hatfield men, still heavily armed, pose with the women in the family. Devil Anse and his wife Louvicy Chafin Hatfield are seated in front. The baby on Louvicy's lap may be Willis.

Several members of the Hatfield clan pose in front of what is believed to be an outbuilding on the Hatfield family home place in Sarah Ann, West Virginia.

In this photo, five Hatfield men are thought to be posed taking target practice near a fence on the Hatfield home place in Sarah Ann. The Hatfield family cemetery begins just a few yards up the steep slope in front of them.

Roseanna McCoy, one of Randall McCoy's daughters, was thought to have been one of the loveliest women in the Tug Valley area. During an 1880 election-day celebration attended by hundreds of local citizens, she caught the eye of Johnson "Johnse" Hatfield, one of Devil Anse's elder sons. Roseanna was believed to be around 19 when she met smooth-talking Johnse. Although the two would live together in the home of Devil Anse, they never married. This caused Roseanna considerable unhappiness, and in 1881, she returned home.

The McCoys took Roseanna back in, but made it clear that her traitorous behavior would forever mark her as disloyal. With her unhappiness mounting, Roseanna moved in with her more understanding Aunt Betty. Despite her ill treatment at the hands of Johnse, she quickly resumed her relationship with him, as depicted in this photo from the 1949 film "Roseanna McCoy." The McCoy men soon devised a way to put an end to the relationship.

The next time the lovers met, several of the McCoy men burst into their Aunt Betty's cabin and took Johnse captive on a trumped-up charge of moonshining. Afraid for Johnse's life, Roseanna borrowed a neighbor's horse and rode through the night to alert the Hatfield clan. Over the years, Roseanna's "Midnight Ride" to save the man she loved has become one of the more romantic elements attributed to the feud.

DID YOU KNOW?

This fanciful pen-and-ink sketch depicts a romanticized Roseanna McCoy during her famous ride to alert her family's sworn enemies about Johnse Hatfield's capture by her brothers. It is highly unlikely, however, that Roseanna took the time to don a full English-style riding habit (popular with fashionable women of the English aristocracy) or that she made her dangerous midnight ride upon a ladylike sidesaddle.

Due to Roseanna's bravado, Devil Anse Hatfield was able to rescue his son. But Johnse "repaid" the now-pregnant Roseanna's loyalty by abandoning her completely and marrying her cousin Nancy. According to family lore, Roseanna soon lost Johnse's baby daughter to fever, with herself dying the following year. This Romeo-and-Juliet story immediately captured the imagination of the country, and it was translated in stories, songs and movies.

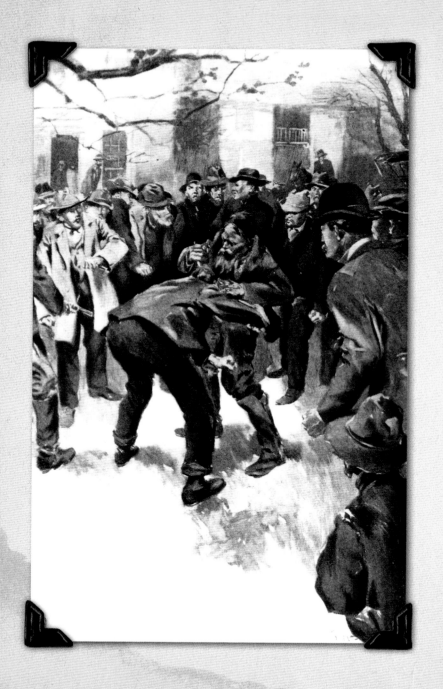

In small 19th-century communities, an election day was a cause for gathering and celebrating. Such was the case in the summer of 1882. However, instead of celebrating, Ellison Hatfield, Devil Anse's brother, got into a fistfight with Tolbert, Pharmer and Bud McCoy, three of Randall's sons. After a brief scuffle, some of the McCoys pulled out knives, and Ellison was stabbed 27 times before being shot in the back. Devil Anse and a posse intercepted the McCoy brothers as they were being taken to a Kentucky jail and escorted them back to West Virginia. Ellison was still alive and, according to Devil Anse, the three McCoys would live only if his brother survived.

In the only photo of Ellison Hatfield known to exist, we see a young Ellison as he appeared when he joined Confederate forces during the Civil War. The image was reproduced for his 1882 funeral, with the caption "Gone but Not Forgotten."

This pen-and-ink drawing depicting the election-day stabbing
death of Ellison Hatfield by the young McCoy brothers
appeared in the book "American Vendetta." This popular
and highly lurid account of the Hatfield-McCoy hostilities
titillated staid Victorian readers and became a best seller.

Soon after Devil Anse Hatfield kidnapped the McCoy brothers to await news of Ellison's recovery, he was visited by the boys' frantic mother, Sarah. After begging on her knees for her sons' lives, an unmoved Devil Anse would only promise that if his brother did not die, he would hand the boys over to the police and that he would bring them back to Kentucky alive. Devil Anse allowed Sarah 10 minutes with her sons before sending her home. The following day, Ellison died of his wounds.

EXECUTION OF THE
THREE M'COY BOYS.

On Aug. 10, 1882, the news spread throughout the valley that Ellison Hatfield had died. Thinking, perhaps that they were being handed over to the authorities, the three McCoy boys were led back to Kentucky by their Hatfield captors. They crossed the Tug River at Matawan, West Virginia, to the Kentucky side. It was there that the Hatfield posse bound the McCoys to some nearby pawpaw trees. Moments later, some 50 rounds were fired into the young men. Devil Anse Hatfield had kept his promise to Sarah McCoy - he had brought her sons back to Kentucky alive.

The murders of Bud, Tolbert and Pharmer McCoy by several members of the Hatfield family during what would become known in Hatfield-McCoy lore as the "Pawpaw Tree Killings" shocked the nation for its brutality and vigilante-style justice.

DID YOU KNOW?

Alexander Messer, a Hatfield family friend, was one of the men involved in the 1882 Pawpaw Tree Killings. Messer was the executioner reportedly responsible for shooting Randall McCoy Jr. In 1888, he was captured in Big Ugly, West Virginia, and sentenced to life in prison. Despite this, Messer was paroled in 1906 but he was sent back to prison that same year for violating his parole. He died in jail in 1922 at the age of 85.

Although unsubstantiated, this photo, now in the collection of the Kentucky Historical Society, purports to show several members of the Hatfield clan displaying the bullet-ridden bodies of Tolbert, Bud and Pharmer McCoy before the corpses were remitted back to their family for burial.

In 1944, 62 years after the McCoy brothers had been shot in retaliation for the death of Ellison Hatfield, *Life* magazine revisited the area the feud had raged so strongly. This photo ran the caption, "Tug Fork is a little stream which divides West Virginia (left) from Kentucky (right). Near this spot three McCoys – Tolbert, Pharmer and Little Randall (Bud) – were tied to pawpaw bushes and killed in cold blood to revenge the stabbing of Ellison Hatfield."

Later in the summer of 1882, Cap Hatfield (seen here in a period drawing), Devil Anse's son, broke into the home of Mary McCoy Daniels, who was purported to be one of the area's most active gossips. Once inside, he savagely whipped Mary and her daughter with a recently butchered cow's tail. Even though she was married to a Hatfield relation, Cap was certain that Mary was sharing damning information – perhaps concerning the pawpaw tree killings – with her McCoy relatives. Her brother, Jeff McCoy, tried to seek revenge for the whippings. He was promptly shot to death on the banks of the Tug River.

For decades, the Tug Fork of the Big Sandy River served as a natural boundary line between the feuding Hatfields of West Virginia and the McCoys of Kentucky. It was at a spot not unlike this one pictured that in 1882 Cap Hatfield shot down Jeff McCoy when he attempted to seek revenge for the "cow tail whipping" of his sister, Mary McCoy Daniels.

By 1887, the multitude of Randall McCoy's real and trumped-up wrongs against the Hatfields had mounted. It was during this year that "Ole Ran'l" turned to his influential political ally, attorney Perry Cline, for help – the very man who had lost 5,000 acres to Devil Anse Hatfield back in 1878. Cline appealed to Kentucky's governor, who lost no time in appointing special officer "Bad" Frank Phillips (left) to apprehend the murderers of the McCoy brothers. To better ensure success, the governor then offered a significant reward, hoping to attract all professional bounty hunters from both sides of the Big Sandy River.

Considered to be a war hero throughout Kentucky for his participation in both the Mexican and American Civil Wars, Simon Bolivar Buckner was elected to the office of governor in 1887. Almost immediately his administration was rocked by the negative publicity that the escalating violence of the Hatfield-McCoy feud was bringing to his state. Like most Kentucky citizens, he had heard of the iron-will reputation of Frank Phillips, and knew this was perhaps the only man that could ferret out the Hatfields responsible for the McCoy brothers' murders.

The feud reached its peak during the now-infamous "New Year's Massacre." During the early morning hours of Jan. 1, 1888, several members of the Hatfield clan, led by Devil Anse's uncle Jim Vance, surrounded the McCoy cabin and began firing rounds into the structure while the family slept. The cabin was then set ablaze in an attempt to drive Randall McCoy into the open. The old man made a break for it, and managed to hide in a nearby corn crib. Two of his children, son Calvin and crippled daughter Alifair, were shot trying to flee. When elderly Sarah McCoy ran from the house toward her dying daughter, she was savagely bludgeoned with a rifle butt by Vance, and left for dead.

This image, which appeared in the *Louisville Courier* in 1888, is thought to be the only image in existence of Randall McCoy's wife, Sarah. After being beaten by Jim Vance, she was dragged away from the burning cabin by the surviving McCoy daughters, and revived. She was never examined by a doctor, but family stories passed down over the years lead historians to believe that the attack left her brain damaged and partially paralyzed. Her exact date of death is unknown, but most surviving McCoys place it around 1890, two years after the beating.

One of Devil Anse's most trusted lieutenants during the family feud was son William Anderson "Cap" Hatfield. Cap learned many of his violent ways from his great uncle, Jim Vance, whom he assisted in planning and executing the New Year's Massacre of the McCoy family. After the raid, he was arrested and jailed, but managed to escape and hide out on a rocky crag called The Devil's Backbone near his family home. He is posed here many years later with friends, showing photographers the exact spot he hid to elude authorities.

Despite his status as a wanted murderer, Cap Hatfield went on to lead a fairly respectable life. In middle age, he studied law via a correspondence course and returned to Logan County hoping to practice with his stepson, attorney Joe Glenn (pictured standing). Just a few days before his death in 1930, the *New York Times* reported: "Concern is felt for William Anderson "Cap" Hatfield, most famous living figure in the famed Hatfield-McCoy feud of the last century, who is ill at his home on Main Island Creek, WV. He is suffering stomach malady and complications, according to physicians. Among those visiting his bedside during the week were Senator Henry D. Hatfield, of Huntington, United States senator and cousin of the sick man. He will likely visit here again during the week-end. 'Cap' Hatfield is the oldest son of 'Devil Anse' Hatfield, outstanding figure in the feud. He is an elder brother of Sheriff Joe Hatfield of this county and Tennis S. Hatfield, former Logan sheriff, and the father of Police Judge Coleman Hatfield, Magistrate L.W. Hatfield and Deputy Sheriff Bob Hatfield, all of this county."

In 1889, W.T. Crawford's book *American Vendetta* was published. Many of the drawings appearing in the book – and subsequent ones like it – fueled the public's misconceptions about Appalachian dwellers. Here, Crawford shows his perception of a "typical mountain girl," in his mind probably not at all unlike the murdered Alifair McCoy.

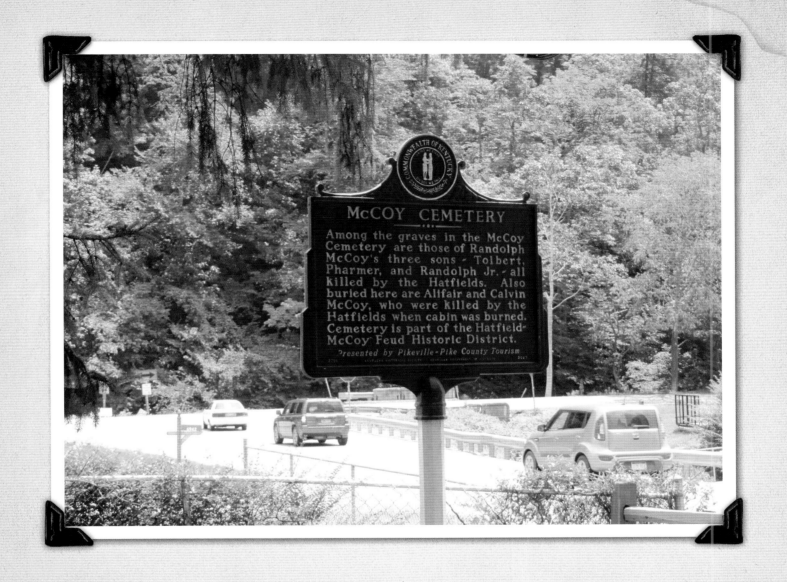

On the marker:

McCOY CEMETERY

Among the graves in the McCoy Cemetery are those of Randolph McCoy's three sons - Tolbert, Pharmer, and Randolph Jr. - all killed by the Hatfields. Also buried here are Alifair and Calvin McCoy, who were killed by the Hatfields when cabin was burned. Cemetery is part of the Hatfield-McCoy Feud Historic District.

Presented by Pikeville-Pike County Tourism

This historical marker in Pike County, Kentucky, informs visitors about the McCoy family cemetery. The names of Alifair and Calvin McCoy – and those of their slain brothers Pharmer, Tolbert and Randolph Jr. – are displayed prominently.

This image of Calvin McCoy's isolated and crudely carved gravestone was taken by a *Life* magazine photographer in 1944. Even after over 60 years had passed since Calvin's death, the feud that had waged in the Tug Valley region still had the ability to capture the public's imagination in a national magazine.

COMMONWEALTH OF KENTUCKY
UNITED WE STAND
DIVIDED WE FALL

SITE OF
RANDOLPH McCOY HOUSE

House was located on Blackberry
Fork of Pond Creek. It burned
Jan. 1, 1888, during a Hatfield
raid. Two of Randolph's children,
Alifair and Calvin, were killed
in attack; their mother Sally was
badly injured. Randolph and other
children escaped. Site is part of
Hatfield-McCoy Feud Historic Dist.
Presented by Pikeville-Pike County Tourism
2001   KENTUCKY HISTORICAL SOCIETY   KENTUCKY DEPARTMENT OF HIGHWAYS   2062

It was said that after the terrible 1888 massacre of his family, Randall McCoy was something of a broken man. He never rebuilt his home, but moved his family to the relative safety of Pikesville, the county seat of Pike County, Kentucky. This historic plaque marks the site where Alifair and Calvin McCoy were murdered and the McCoy homestead burned to the ground.

Most historians agree that Devil Anse Hatfield may have helped to organize the New Year's Massacre of 1888, but that he did not physically participate. It is possible, however, that he lent his firearms, including this revolver, to those involved.

The date of this photo is unknown, but it may very well have been taken around the time of the New Year's Massacre at The Devil's Backbone, the Hatfield family hideout, immediately following the murders of Calvin and Alifair McCoy. Here we see Hatfield family employee Ock Damron, Devil Anse and his uncle Jim Vance, the man responsible for masterminding the attack, and for beating Sarah McCoy senseless and leaving her for dead. Ten days after the murders, "Bad" Frank Phillips shot and killed Vance.

On Jan. 18, 1888, less than three weeks after the McCoy cabin was burned to the ground in West Virginia, Frank Phillips organized a raiding party of nearly 40 men to illegally enter Kentucky to round up the Hatfields responsible for the recent murders. He was especially hopeful of arresting Devil Anse Hatfield. Phillips' posse was met by a group of Kentucky men, all angered that a West Virginia posse dared to challenge the sovereignty of their native state. The ensuing skirmish, today called the Battle of Grapevine Creek, did not result in substantive gains for either side of the feud.

The son of murdered unionist Asa Harmon McCoy, Bud McCoy, had for years refused any involvement in the Hatfield-McCoy feud. However, his attitude changed after his brother Jeff was killed on the banks of the Tug River by Cap Hatfield while trying to avenge his sister's beating with a severed cow tail. Bud McCoy was the only man wounded at the Battle of Grapevine Creek.

DID YOU KNOW?

A posse of McCoy sympathizers met members of the Hatfield clan at Grapevine Creek. According to an 1888 newspaper account, "After crossing the river the McCoys . . . were fired upon by a squad of eight from the Hatfield gang . . . The capturing party immediately returned the fire, and Will Dempsey, of the Hatfield gang, fell to the ground shot through the bowels. At this juncture the Hatfields beat a hasty retreat, throwing away their blankets, overcoats, etc. The posse went up to where Dempsey was although he was in a dying condition and begged piteously to be saved as he would not live long, despite his cries for mercy, the man that killed Jim Vance on the first raid put his gun against Dempsey's head and almost blew it off."

Soon after the Battle of Grapevine Creek, Devil Anse's elder brother, Valentine "Wall" Hatfield, and eight others were arrested by another marauding Kentucky posse led by Frank Phillips. The men were brought to Kentucky to stand trial for the murder of Alifair and Calvin McCoy, but only after spending months haggling over state extradition issues concerning the legality of their arrest. All would be found guilty. This sketch is of the Pikeville jail.

Wall Hatfield, a former Logan County judge, gave himself up to Frank Phillips, fully believing that his brother's powerful political connections could quickly set him free. But after the 1888 New Year's Massacre, the tide of opinion had drastically changed, and the Hatfields soon found themselves the target of a mighty backlash from the citizens on both sides of the Big Sandy River. Wall was sentenced to life imprisonment for his participation in the massacre, and died in jail 20 years later.

Lark McCoy, pictured here with his wife Elizabeth in 1904, was part of Frank Phillips' posse that entered Kentucky and killed Jim Vance. Some said it was divine retribution, because nearly 25 years earlier, Vance had shot and killed his father, Asa Harmon McCoy. It was also rumored that Lark dipped his handkerchief in Vance's blood and proceeded to polish his boots. Less than a week later, Lark also participated in the Battle of Grapevine Creek, which marked the official end to the feud.

The Pike County courthouse in Pikeville, Kentucky, was where members of the Hatfield clan were tried and found guilty of murdering Calvin and Alifair McCoy. Seven of those standing trial received terms of life imprisonment. The eighth, Ellison "Cottontop" Mounts – Ellison Hatfield's illegitimate son – was sent to the gallows a year after the trial in 1890. According to period reports, Mounts was said to have been an albino and "severely dim-witted." To this day, many thought the possibly mentally handicapped boy was tricked into confessing that his was the shot that killed 15-year-old Alifair. Most historians agree that it was likely Cap Hatfield who fired the fatal shot.

PIKE CO. COURTHOUSE AND JAIL

Courthouse erected 1888-89 by McDonald Bros.; later renovated 1932-33. Here was scene of Hatfield clan trials for murders of Tolbert, Randolph, Jr., Pharmer, Alifair and Calvin McCoy. The defendants lodged in adjacent jail; found guilty and sentenced to life in prison except Ellison Mounts, hanged February 18, 1890. Courthouse and jail part of Hatfield-McCoy Feud Historic Dist.

1990   KENTUCKY HISTORICAL SOCIETY   KENTUCKY DEPARTMENT OF HIGHWAYS   1866

KEEP

Today, this historic marker can be found outside the Pikeville courthouse to commemorate the site of the infamous Hatfield trial that officially ended one of the bloodiest family feuds in U.S. history.

Media interest in the feud lingered for many years after the hanging of Ellison Mounts in 1890. During this time, Devil Anse Hatfield and his family kept mainly to themselves, rarely straying from the family homestead in Sarah Ann, West Virginia. Here, Devil Anse and wife Louvicy sit on the large front porch of their home around 1900, posing for curious photographers, while surrounded by some of their children who had managed to escape imprisonment.

During most of the 1890s, Devil Anse felt he and his family would be safer from vigilantes in the more remote area of Main Island Creek, Kentucky, only returning to the family homestead in Sarah Ann sometime around 1900. Here, he and Louvicy stare at the camera from in front of the large Hatfield house after their return to Sarah Ann. By 1900, several of their nine sons were either incarcerated, on the lam, or dead. Devil Anse remained wanted by the law for the 1888 deaths of Alifair and Calvin McCoy, but he was never prosecuted.

By the 1900s, the world that Devil Anse Hatfield and his family had been born into had changed drastically. The clannish, isolated world that most of the old mountaineers had grown up with was eroding, and the modern world was forcing itself in. Most families, the Hatfields included, could only look on with sadness as the area began to fall victim to full-scale deforestation from the timber industry and the negative influences of strip mining for coal. Less than 10 years after the great Hatfield-McCoy feud had ended, the people living on the banks of the Big Sandy River could no longer shut out the wholesale industrialization that would characterize the area in the decades to come.

In his waning years, Devil Anse lived out his life quietly by going hunting for small game, making whiskey and doing some old-style logging with his younger sons. On rare occasions he would go to the Logan County courthouse to vote, chat with his friend H.C. Ragland of the *Logan Banner* or to visit his brother Elias, now working as a deputy sheriff. Ragland always made a point of mentioning when Devil Anse visited town, but nearly always limited his editorial comments to their conversations about the supply of game animals in the region.

In 1911, at the age of 73, Devil Anse Hatfield shocked his friends, family and neighbors by announcing that he had underwent a religious rediscovery and had decided to be baptized. In October of that year, he underwent the baptismal ceremony by stepping into the brisk waters of Main Island Creek, not far from the Hatfield homestead in Sarah Ann. One relative who attended the ceremony claimed that Devil Anse had not yet jettisoned all of his old ways, as the handle of a pistol could be clearly seen protruding from the waistband of his trousers.

No one was more surprised by Devil Anse's desire for religious conversion than hardline preacher "Uncle Dyke" Garrett of the Logan Church of Christ. Despite their religious differences, the two disparate men became friends and developed a mutual respect for each other. Garrett had served with Devil Anse during the Civil War with the Logan Wildcats. Later, he was active with him in the Camp Stratton United Confederate Veterans – an organization heavily involved in area politics until 1915 when its elderly membership began dying out. He is pictured here about 10 years after he performed the 1911 baptism, posing with Anse's daughter-in-law, Mrs. Willis Hatfield.

On Oct. 17, 1911, Detroit and Elias Hatfield became the first of Devil Anse's sons to pass away – nearly 25 years after the Hatfield-McCoy feud had ended. An Italian named Octavio Jerome killed the brothers in Boomer, West Virginia, during a fight over liquor distribution interests. The Hatfields claimed Jerome was encroaching upon their saloon-owner customers by offering cheaper alcoholic products. When the brothers confronted Jerome, shots were fired and all three men were fatally wounded.

By 1911, most of Devil Anse's sons were jailed or had spent some significant time behind bars, but despite the bloody feud that had raged throughout the 1880s, none of his children had been killed. The death of two of his younger boys came as a shock. Rumors spread like wildfire that the old mountaineer might gather a posse to take vengeance upon the growing Italian immigrant population then working in the coal mines. However, this scenario never materialized.

Henry D. Hatfield was one of Devil Anse's many grandchildren. Henry's father, Elias Hatfield, was one of Anse's sons to be charged with the murder of Tolbert, Bud and Pharmer McCoy during the pawpaw tree incident in 1882. Henry earned a medical degree, served as a state senator, and eventually won a bid for governor.

DID YOU KNOW?

"Henry Drury Hatfield was born on Mate Creek in present Mingo County, the son of a Confederate soldier and relative of Anderson 'Devil Anse' Hatfield. He graduated from Franklin College at age fifteen and received his medical degree from the University of Louisville at age nineteen. In 1904, Hatfield received a second medical degree, with a specialization in surgery, from New York University. He worked as a railroad division surgeon, mine physician, and as Mingo County health commissioner. Due to the lack of proper health facilities in southwestern West Virginia, Hatfield appealed to the legislature, which appropriated funds for the Miners Hospital No. 1 in Welch, McDowell County. After serving briefly on the McDowell County Court, he was elected to the state senate and was chosen as its president in 1911." — West Virginia Division of Culture and History

SPEAKING OF
Dr. H.D. HATFIELD
BECKLEY. W.VA.
NOV. 1. 1912

By 1912, many of Elias' sons had prospered and become respectable citizens, and none more so than Henry D. Hatfield, who was voted in as Republican governor of West Virginia. Crowds of voters are pictured waiting for Hatfield to make an appearance and deliver his acceptance speech at the state capitol building in Beckley, West Virginia.

SPEAKING BY
Dr. H.D. HATFIELD
BECKLEY W.VA. NOV. 1-12.

Before serving as governor, Henry Hatfield was a state senator from 1908 to 1912. Although obstructed by a tree, here he addresses a crowd of admirers after securing the office of governor of West Virginia soon after the November 1912 elections. When his term was over in 1917, he joined the army during WWI as a major in the U.S. Medical Corps. He retired from politics in the late 1930s.

During the summer of 1914, the tiny coal town of Glen Alum in Mingo County, West Virginia, was rocked by the news that three men transporting a company payroll of $7,000 had been shot to death on an arriving train. After the murders had been committed, the robbers vanished into the nearby hills. Later that day, Sheriff Greenway Hatfield, a nephew of Devil Anse, assembled his deputies to organize a manhunt. Sheriff Hatfield, his hat in hand, crouches third from right in the front row beside the fallen tree where the bandits were eventually apprehended and killed.

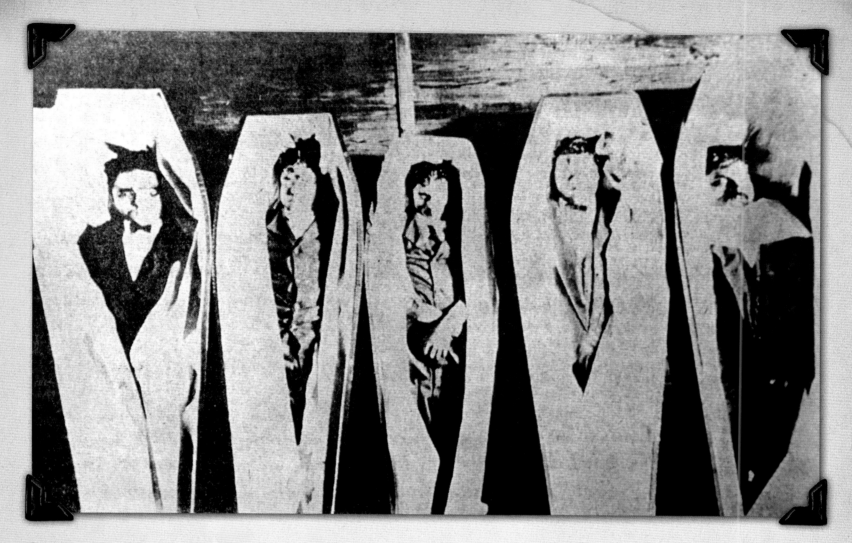

For two days the Glen Alum bandits were pursued by a posse of nearly 50 men. When the bandits finally stopped to stand their ground, an hour-long gunfight ensued. According to a local newspaper account, "the advancing law men discovered that the stronghold of the bandits was a fallen tree. They also discovered that the bandits were not natives, as had been suspected, but . . . Italians. When the law men reached the lair of the bandits, they found that only one of the five had survived the night. The bodies of all of them were riddled with bullets. Who killed the living bandit was never definitely established, nor were other facts about the brutal crime." The bodies of the dead men were laid out in the nearby town of Williamson, West Virginia, to be viewed by thousands of curious locals.

Very few images of Randall McCoy are known to exist. He is pictured here with wife Sarah in an 1888 drawing that appeared in the *Louisville Courier*. Unlike his nemesis Devil Anse Hatfield, Randall McCoy lost five of his children to the bloody feuding that raged around the Big Sandy River back in the 1880s. Many say that by the early 1910s, he had become an embittered and unstable man. In 1914, the following article appeared in a Mingo County newspaper: "Pineville, KY, Jan. 9 – Randall McCoy is dying. He is one of the best known men in the mountains and was a leader in the noted McCoy-Hatfield feud of some years ago which resulted in a score of deaths. His condition is a result of burns he sustained when he fell into an open fireplace while making coffee at the home of his grandson. Before assistance could reach him, his clothes had been burnt from his body. He is eight-six years of age. The doctors say he cannot survive the day."

MCCOY

SARAH
1829 — 189—

RANDOLPH
1825 — 1914

FAMED LEADER, HATFIELD—McCOY FUED

Just days after the tragic cooking fire accident that would take his life in 1914, Randolph McCoy died at the age of 88, not 86 as stated in the newspaper article. Sometime during the 1970s, his worn and faded headstone was replaced with this handsome granite marker that he shares with his wife, Sarah. They are buried in the Dils Cemetery in Pikeville.

William Sidney Hatfield was the great nephew of Devil Anse. By 1920, the 30-year-old had been appointed police chief of Matewan, West Virginia. A staunch supporter of the coalminer unions, Hatfield made an attempt to prevent Albert and Lee Felts – men hired by the mining company – from evicting itinerate mine workers from their homes.

A shootout ensued, today known as the Matewan Massacre, and five people were dead, including the Felts brothers.

Mary Harris Jones, commonly known as "Mother Jones," was an outspoken activist for American labor interests, especially for the United Mine Workers. When she came to Mingo County, West Virginia, in the late 1910s to speak against the terrible wages and working conditions that coalminers were facing, she posed in this photograph with several town leaders. Sheriff Sid Hatfield, third from left, reportedly was an ardent admirer of the older lady.

Over a year had passed since the Matewan gun battle, but the mining company arranged to have William Hatfield indicted on murder charges stemming from the shootout that resulted in the deaths of the Felts brothers. In 1921, he was acquitted of the charges by a jury. Later that year, he was sent to stand trial with Ed Chambers (seen here with Hatfield) on conspiracy charges for an unrelated incident. Hatfield was unarmed when several men seeking revenge for the death of the Felts brothers shot and killed both Hatfield and Chambers on the steps of the McDowell County Courthouse in Welch, West Virginia.

This photo of the McDowell County Courthouse was taken soon after the Hatfield-Chambers murders. The exact spot of the execution can be seen on the photo marked with a small "X." Newspaper reports revealed that the unarmed Hatfield had been shot 17 times. No one was ever charged in Hatfield's assassination.

Jessie Lee Hatfield and Lucinda Chambers were standing at their husbands' sides when the two men were assaulted and murdered on the McDowell County Courthouse steps early in 1921. Here, they smile for cameras while wearing full-mourning dresses in front of the Capitol Building during the U.S. Senate investigation into the murders.

Lucinda Chambers and Jessie Lee Hatfield pose in 1921 with Mrs. Mooney (center), wife of leading mine workers unionist Frank Mooney, soon after their return to West Virginia. Lucinda and Jessie Lee were the only witnesses to their husbands' murders, and the Mooneys were very concerned for the widows' safety after the investigation was concluded. They need not have feared, because no suspects for the killings were ever brought to trial.

Believed to have been taken around 1928, this photo shows cousins Crockett and Cap Hatfield playing with one of several tame bear cubs raised by Devil Anse on his property in Sarah Ann, West Virginia.

Here, the old man looks on amused as his son and nephew gaze upon the treed bear.

Devil Anse Hatfield
and Wife

Taken around 1918, this is thought to be one of the last photos showing Devil Anse and Levicy Hatfield posing together. By the time Devil Anse died in 1921, he and Levicy had been married for 60 years and raised 13 children.

DID YOU KNOW?

Levicy Hatfield was probably a classic Appalachian Mountains wife. In an article appearing in Tennessee's *LaFollett Press*, Dallas Bogan wrote of mountain marriages: "It was deemed inappropriate for the wives to be seen while the men were eating. They would prepare the food, set the table and return to the kitchen while the men absorbed the fine meal. The women would eat their meals in the kitchen. Women were seldom seen out in public and, if they were, they always stayed beside or behind their husbands . . . It was customary to find most wives pregnant, they having a baby a year . . . Many Appalachian women became so fatigued from having babies that they would die at an early age. It wasn't rare for a man to have had three or four wives and thirty or forty children."

When he passed away from complications due to pneumonia in 1921, William Anderson "Devil Anse" Hatfield was 82 years old. His death was big news in Logan County, and it was attended by hundreds of people. His immediate family pose here with the open casket, from left to right: Thelma Latelle LaFollett, Mrs. Elliott Hatfield, Nancy "Sis" Hatfield Vance, Rose Hatfield Browning, Mrs. Anderson Hatfield, Tennis Hatfield, Elliott Mitchel, Elizabeth Hatfield Caldwell, Jonse Hatfield, Smith Hatfield, Emma Smith, Elea Hatfield, C.A. Hatfield, "Cap" Hatfield, Bob Hatfield, Dr. Elliott Hatfield, Muriel Hatfield Beres, Joe Wolfe, Ples Browning and the Cook boys.

A large, impressive house by Sarah Ann standards, the Hatfield home had become increasingly run down after the trials held in 1888. During the vigilante-raiders period, the house had been transformed into a literal fortress, even sporting a medieval-style moat and drawbridge. By the time of Devil Anse's death in 1921, it was reported to be in a near state of collapse. However, Levicy Hatfield refused to leave the home where she had raised 13 children.

Devil Anse's funeral was a big attraction in Logan County, and some reports claimed that nearly 1,000 locals came to pay their final respects to him at the Hatfield family house. In more ways than one, his death marked an end of an era. By 1920, the lifestyles of the old mountain families had changed forever. Sarah Ann, no longer a rural backwater, was now dominated by coal mining and now stood adjacent to a thriving industrial hub.

In 1922, a year after the death of Devil Anse, the Hatfield clan gathered for a family reunion to dedicate a fine marble memorial (carved in Italy) to their undisputed, but now gone, patriarch. Here, crowds listen to the various speeches given by family members at the base of a steep slope in front of the Hatfield house. The dirt road pictured leads up to the Hatfield family cemetery.

The life-sized marble statue of Devil Anse was commissioned his surviving children and bears a striking resemblance to him. Here we see Levicy, still wearing a mourning dress a year after her husband's death, posing with her extended family beside the new monument. She insisted that the names of all her children be carved into the base of the memorial.

Levicy Hatfield agrees to once again be photographed in front of the new memorial to her dead husband. She is seen here standing at center flanked by two of her daughters. Levicy and Devil Anse had been married for 60 years at the time of his death.

The memorial to Devil Anse is now over 90 years old, and the old Hatfield family cemetery has become a bit neglected and overgrown. Somewhat battered and weather-stained, the monument still remains one of the best likenesses of the fallen mountaineer. The grave is visited by countless tourists who continue to be fascinated by the bloody family feud.

In early June 1927, an Associated Press newswire story appeared under the headline "Last Survivors of Celebrated Feud Now Pals" along with this image of Bob McCoy and Joe Hatfield shaking hands. The story read, "The bitter feud that raged a generation ago between the Hatfields and McCoys, in which 35 men and one woman were killed in the Kentucky and West Virginia mountains, has ended. Here are Bob McCoy (left), of Wyoming County, W.Va., and Joe Hatfield, of Mingo County, W.Va. They are fellow students at Marshall College, Huntington, fraternity brothers and regular pals."

The AP newswire story claiming that Bob McCoy and Joe Hatfield were the last survivors of the feud was hardly accurate. At the time the photo on the preceding page was taken, dozens of members from both clans were certainly still living – many in the very region of the feud. In this circa-1920s image, Devil Anse's youngest sons, Tennyson "Tennis" (left) and Emanuel "Willis" Hatfield are seen posing with Tennyson's wife, Sadie. Tennyson died in 1953 and Willis, the last surviving child of Devil Anse, passed away in 1978.

DID YOU KNOW?

When Willis Hatfield died in 1978, the Associated Press wrote: "Hatfield was the 12th of 13 children born to the infamous clan chieftain and his wife, Levicy Chafin Hatfield. He grew up in a log house on Main Island Creek in Logan County in West Virginia, and until his death could recite tales of the fussin' and feudin' between the two clans . . . As for the McCoys, Willis Hatfield says he bears no grudges."

This photo of Levicy and Devil Anse Hatfield and is thought to date to about 1918, just a few years before Devil Anse's death in 1921. Louvisa "Levicy" Chafin Hatfield did not last out the decade, passing away herself in Logan County on March 15, 1929. Little is known of Levicy, as she is thought to have been illiterate, and no writings of hers are known to exist. In 1888, during the height of the feud, journalist T.C. Crawford of the *New York World* interviewed Devil Anse in the Hatfield house. All Crawford noted of Devil Anse's wife was, "Levicy Hatfield's small dark eyes shone with matronly pride when her husband talked of his escapades in the feud."

After hearing the final rites being read over her freshly dug grave, the last of the mourners paying their final respects to Levicy Hatfield file past the memorial of her husband as they slowly make their way downhill to join a sizeable funeral motorcade. Levicy, matriarch of the large Hatfield clan, passed away quietly in 1929 of natural causes at the age of 87.

Known as "The Traipsin' Woman," photographer Jean Thomas traveled the eastern Kentucky mountains taking candid snapshots that recorded the mountain way of life. Thomas was just a small child during the 1880s – the bloodiest years of the Hatfield-McCoy feud – but she had grown up listening to the stories of the main participants. By the time she took this 1942 photo of feudist descendants Asa Harmon "Bud" McCoy (left) and Grover Cleveland Hatfield, most of the facts surrounding the feud had passed into the realm of legend.

Bud McCoy discusses the details of a local political petition with his Canonsburg neighbor, Grover Hatfield. In a strange twist of fate, both men were closely linked to the events surrounding the feud a generation earlier. Bud was the grandson of Asa Harmon McCoy, the man put to death by the Logan County Wildcats for his Union sympathies during the Civil War. Grover was the great-grandson of Anderson "Preacher Anse" Hatfield, Devil Anse's cousin and the judge who had presided over the famous Hog Trial back in 1878.

"Traipsin' Woman" photographer Jean Thomas was fascinated by the music, crafts and language patterns of eastern Kentucky, and spent years traveling the region to create a photographic record. She was particularly involved in helping to stage the annual American Folk Song Festival. Many of her best-known images include people involved in quilting, basket making and other crafts. This is particularly true when it came to scenes with community and family groups. Here, Bud McCoy and his youngest son show off their skills with the banjo while his wife Rhoda proudly displays one of her prize quilts.

In this rare color photo (Jean Thomas rarely used color film) Bud McCoy picks off a tune on his banjo. Thomas was passionate about recording the folk songs of the region, and today many of her mid-century recordings are preserved at the University of Louisville.

DID YOU KNOW?

According to Debby McClatchy in *Appalachian Music: A Short History*: "Traditional Appalachian music is mostly based upon anglo-celtic folk ballads and instrumental dance tunes. The former were almost always sung unaccompanied, and usually by women, fulfilling roles as keepers of the families' cultural heritages and rising above dreary monotonous work through fantasies of escape and revenge. These ballads were from the British tradition of the single personal narrative, but the list was selective; most of the one hundred or so variations of the three hundred classic ballads found in American tradition are to do with sexual struggles from the female standpoint such as, *Lord Thomas and Fair Ellender*, and *Pretty Polly*."

In this 1942 image, we find Bud McCoy and his youngest son posing for Jean Thomas beside the well on their Canonsburg, Kentucky, farm. Bud was reported to have been reticent about discussing his personal connection to the feud that had ended nearly 50 years earlier, but there are several interviews and photos that seem to contradict this.

DID YOU KNOW?

Bud McCoy's family dog appears to be a Mountain Feist. The Feist is a breed typically found in the Ozark and Appalachian mountain regions of the United States. Often mistaken for a rat terrier or a Jack Russell terrier, the Feist is small and agile, and perfectly suited to hunting and tracking in mountainous terrains. Abraham Lincoln referred to the Feist in a poem he wrote during the early days of his presidency, and George Washington mentioned the "hunting Feist" in diary entries.

Bud's wife Rhoda, posing here for Thomas with her daughters, was one of the region's most skilled quilters. Well into the 20th century, quilting – and participating in quilting bees – was one of the best social outlets for women in the more remote regions of eastern Kentucky. In an economically depressed area, the creation of such quilts for the tourist trade could provide some much needed extra income.

DID YOU KNOW?

"Patches of family history will show up in the quilts made by women throughout Appalachian regions. A quilt is much like a scrapbook of times past. Grandma's old favorite dress, Grandpa's favorite shirt, fabric scraps stuffed in an old box Auntie kept for years, worn curtains, fabric from just about any family garment eventually ended up in a quilt. This was the way of quilting for the early settlers of Appalachia country. There is a long history of self-sustainability and resourcefulness in the Appalachian Mountains, and quilting was one of the skills women had to learn."
— *Appalachian Style Quilts*, Phyllis Doyle Burns

Frankie McCoy, great-granddaughter of the murdered Asa Harmon McCoy, was in her late 20s when she posed for this early 1940s photo. She is seen standing center, flanked by two men - one of whom is Devil Anse Hatfield's son Tennyson "Tennis" Hatfield, then the proprietor of a Logan County "gin joint" called The Silver Moon.

DID YOU KNOW?

While some of the older Hatfield brothers ended up serving long jail sentences, Devil Anse's younger sons — including Tennyson — seemed to reach a degree of respectability in the years following the feud. In *West Virginia, a History* by John Alexander Williams, we learn: "While some of Anse's sons continued to lead turbulent lives, most of the younger generation settled down to respectable modes of existence . . . for example: young Willis, after a youthful brush with the law, went to work for a coal firm; Joe became the first Republican sheriff of Logan County in 1924; and, despite the generally scandalous character of his (Joe's) term, was succeeded in office by Tennyson Hatfield."

Frankie McCoy may not have shared her mother Rhoda's skill as a quilt maker, but she was reported to have had a fine singing voice. Here she poses with a group of musical friends, possibly during the annual American Folk Song Festival. Dressing in period clothing popular during the years of the Hatfield-McCoy feud, some of the sung ballads extolled the exploits of the battling mountain families.

DID YOU KNOW?

By the 1940s, some members of old Mingo County families (such as Frankie McCoy) were compelled for financial reasons to swallow their pride and entertain an increasing number of curious tourists, singing old "hillbilly" songs in period costumes. In 2006, T.R.C. Hutton of Vanderbilt University wrote: "Many students of Appalachian history are quite familiar with narratives of exploitation and poverty . . . from brutal Civil War-era guerrilla warfare to coal strikes in which collective bargaining was far rarer than pitched battles between labor and capital to ecological degradation brought about by extractive industries to grinding poverty and then finally the humiliation of the familiar 'hillbilly' stereotype . . . many students of the subject to naturally associate the mountain South with ubiquitous tragedy."

In 1944, *Life* magazine went to Mingo County (formerly named Logan County) to do a follow-up photo essay on the Hatfield-McCoy feud that had ended nearly 55 years earlier. By that time, truth and legend had blurred, and most of the living descendants had no ill feelings concerning their former family enemies. *Life* photographer Walter Sanders accompanied photographer Jean Thomas through the region, and in this photo we see Allen Harkins Hatfield and his wife Nellie McCoy Hatfield. Devil Anse's great uncle Joe was Allen's great-grandfather, and Randall McCoy's uncle Sam was Nellie's great-grandfather.

Landon Lawson Hatfield was nearly 70 years old when *Life* magazine came to Mingo County. He had only been a boy of 13 when his ancestors had stood trial in 1888, but he well remembered stories of the old "stink tree," a hollow oak where the Hatfields supposedly stuffed the bodies of slain McCoys before they could be hidden in unmarked graves. Landon's grandfather Richard was Devil Anse's cousin.

DID YOU KNOW?

In the *Hatfield-McCoy Feud Reader*, Shirley Donnelly connects then-7-year-old Landon Hatfield to the 1882 Pawpaw Tree Incident — one of the bloodiest events of the feud. "On the West Virginia side of the Tug, the Hatfields were mourning for Devil Anse's brother, Ellison Hatfield, who had succumbed Aug. 9 to wounds inflicted two days earlier by Tolbert, Pharmer and Randolph McCoy Jr. . . . Justice had been swift and summary for the brothers there in that fierce region where the stern code of an eye for an eye and a tooth for a tooth had long been regarded as the law of the clans. The place where the three McCoy brothers were shot was pointed out to me on Feb. 14, 1955, by Landon Lawson Hatfield, 79. He was born on Nov. 28, 1875, and was a boy of 7, he said, when he witnessed the bloody scene."

Not too long after the death of Levicy Hatfield, the old Hatfield family house was torn down and replaced with this cluster of sheds and shacks. Backed by steep hills and fronted by Island Creek, the old house had been perfectly situated to repel vigilante attacks during the 1880s and '90s. By 1944, Devil Anse's wooden drawbridge had long ago been replaced with the permanent bridge seen here.

By 1944, only six of Devil Anse and Levicy Hatfield's 13 children were still living. Here, Anse's son Joseph Davis Hatfield visits his father's grave with one of his grandsons. To the left can be seen the twin markers commemorating his brothers Elias and Troy, murdered in 1911, and to the right is his older brother Johnse's marker, erected in 1922.

As WWII was coming to a close, *Life* magazine could show no better example of Americans forgetting their differences and coming together than to portray Hatfield and McCoy descendants working together for the war effort. Here, 17-year-old Shirley Hatfield (preacher Anse Hatfield was her great-uncle) poses with fellow uniform factory worker Frankie McCoy. Frankie's great grandfather was Asa Harmon McCoy, murdered 80 years earlier when the feud first began.

Hatfield and McCoy women gather in the home of Frank McCoy, Bud's brother, in order to put the final touches on a quilt commemorating the war efforts of both families. Stitched into the upper left star are the words "DEVIL ANSE / Cpt. Anderson / HATFIELD / Logan Wildcats / 1863." In the upper right star "Pvt. Harmon McCoy / UNION ARMY / 1863" can be seen. The lower left-hand star has the embroidered words "Pvt. Woodrow McCoy / SON OF / America Hatfield McCoy / '43." The lower right-hand star is stitched "Pvt. / CHARLES D. HATFIELD / SON OF / Toland McCoy Hatfield / 1943."

This 1907 photo was taken soon after the wedding of Bud and Rhoda McCoy. Despite the fact that Bud's grandfather, Asa Harmon McCoy, was killed by the Logan Wildcats and his father, Larkin McCoy, fought during the Battle of Grapevine Creek in 1888, Bud always claimed that he never harbored any ill feelings toward the Hatfield family.

When *Life* magazine photographer Walter Sanders visited Mingo County in 1944, he persuaded Bud and Rhoda to recapture the exact pose of their wedding photo, taken nearly 40 years earlier.

DID YOU KNOW?

Bud McCoy was known to be passionate about preserving the music of the region. His wife Rhoda was equally passionate about the art of quiltmaking. In May 1943, the *Milwaukee Journal* reported on a local folksong festival and said: "One of the featured singers will be Bud McCoy, who will be heard in ballads with his grandson, Little Bud, and Melissy Hatfield. Little Bud, accompanied on the banjo by his grandfather, will sing 'Victory Quilt Ballad.' The song refers to a victory quilt, designed and made by Rhoda McCoy, in which are quilted the names of Devil Anse Hatfield and Randall McCoy, leaders in the once celebrated Hatfield-McCoy feud, and the names of the present generation of both families now in the armed forces. The quilt will be exhibited and later raffled off for war bonds."

After the "Pawpaw Tree Killings" of 1882, the feud simmered as the McCoy family struggled without much success to have the responsible Hatfields arrested and publicly tried in the courts. The governor of Kentucky requested their extradition from West Virginia Gov. E. Willis Wilson, who refused. Throughout the late 1880s, it sometimes seemed armed conflict might arise between the two states. In a show of gratitude, Devil Anse Hatfield named his youngest son after Gov. Wilson. Willis Hatfield was his last surviving son, shown here in 1970 at age 82.

SIX OF THE SIXTEEN CHILDREN
OF RANDOLPH AND SARAH McCOY
LIE BURIED HERE, HAVING SUFFERED
UNTIMELY DEATH.

THREE DIED BOUND TO PAWPAW TREES
AT THE MOUTH OF BLACKBERRY CREEK
IN AUGUST, 1882.

ONE IS BELIEVED TO HAVE DIED OF
GRIEF BECAUSE HIS BROTHER HAD
BEEN SHOT IN HIS STEAD.

TWO PERISHED WHEN THEIR HOME
WAS BURNED IN JANUARY, 1888.
THE HOMESITE IS VISIBLE ACROSS
THE VALLEY ABOVE THIS PLACE.

TOLBERT   1854 — 1882
ALIFAIR   1858 — 1888
CALVIN   1862 — 1888
PHARMER   1863 — 1882
RANDOLPH JR.   1864 — 1882
WILLIAM   1866 —

"THERE IS NO SECRET
WHY THEY DIED SO YOUNG,
PRIDE TOOK CONTROL,
YOUTH'S SONG WAS NEVER SUNG."
                        JIM WOLFORD
                        BOB STANLEY

THIS MARKER PRESENTED
TO THE
PRESERVATION COUNCIL OF PIKE COUNTY
BY THE
McCOY FAMILY
1975

McCOY

In May 1976, this handsome granite McCoy family memorial was dedicated by McCoy descendants Leonard and Joseph McCoy, wealthy coal operators. By a strange twist of fate, the heavy stone marker was delivered to the McCoys by the Hatfield Monument Company of Sarah Ann, West Virginia.

When the new McCoy family memorial was dedicated in the Dils Cemetery in Pikeville, Kentucky, Willis Hatfield (left) was 88 years old. He is seen here posing in front of the marker and shaking hands with 92-year-old Jim "Grandpaw" McCoy. When asked about his family's arch nemesis, Hatfield is reported to have remarked, "Some of those McCoys are pretty good fellows."

According to an article appearing in the *Daytona Beach Morning Journal*, "Hatfield, who was only a youngster during most of the fighting, was standing beside 'Grandpaw' Jim McCoy. McCoy still lives near the home place and says he well remembers the night in 1888 that the Hatfields burned down his family's log cabin and killed two of his cousins. Like Hatfield, McCoy said he also bears no grudge. He said he soon forgave the Hatfields and even drank moonshine with Devil Anse a few years after the burning . . . A buffet luncheon followed the dedication. The two men who remember the feud cut the cake."

In 1979, the Hatfield and McCoy descendants agreed to appear for a special week's taping of the then-popular television game show "Family Feud." They played for a cash prize and a pig (the theft of which reportedly started the feud back in 1878) that was kept caged on stage during the entire taping. The McCoy family emerged victorious, winning three games to two, but the Hatfield family won more money ($11,272 to the McCoys' $8,459). Perhaps to avoid a rekindling of the feud, McCoy family's winnings were increased to $11,273.

"Family Feud" host Richard Dawson looks as if he might be caught
in the middle of a 20th-century rebirth of the old Hatfield-McCoy feud.

In 2012, The History Channel produced a "Hatfields & McCoys" mini-series, and the saga of the warring mountain families soon fascinated a new generation. Film star Kevin Costner was selected to play Devil Anse Hatfield. When asked in a *Huffington Post* interview to draw a modern parallel to the feud, he said, "We certainly had a difficult time recovering from the Civil War ... If someone victimized your family, your sister or brother, you would settle that score. So when we think about Iraq right now, or Pakistan or the Taliban in Afghanistan, and the murder that's going on, these things are going to be settled. And they're going to be settled in the middle of the night with people handcuffed and thrown into ditches ... I mean, we haven't come very far."

Actor Bill Paxton assumed the role of Randall McCoy in the TV mini-series. In the same interview, he reported, "It just shows the circle of violence and how it's perpetuated. It's a biblical story really, a cautionary tale … These people are just haunted people, just haunted as fl@#. Randall McCoy becomes a fanatic, an obsessed fanatic … almost like a jihadist or something. The betrayal of a friend or family member always cuts deeper than if someone slighted you outside of that. And real obsession is a dangerous thing. This guy ate, drank and slept his obsession, and it poisoned his children."

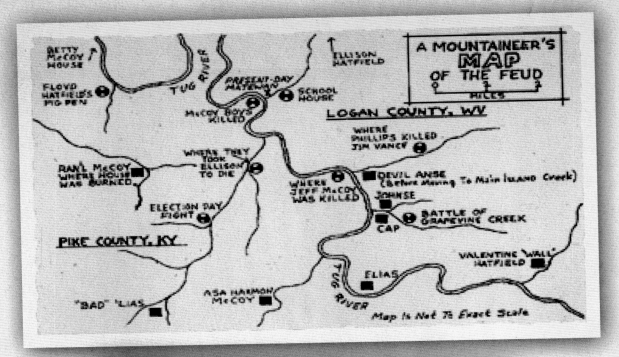

A MOUNTAINEER'S MAP OF THE FEUD

MILES

LOGAN COUNTY, WV

BETTY McCOY HOUSE

ELLISON HATFIELD

FLOYD HATFIELD'S PIG PEN

TUG RIVER

PRESENT-DAY MATEWAN

SCHOOL HOUSE

McCOY BOYS KILLED

WHERE PHILLIPS KILLED JIM VANCE

RAN'L McCOY WHERE HOUSE WAS BURNED

WHERE THEY TOOK ELLISON TO DIE

WHERE JEFF McCOY WAS KILLED

DEVIL ANSE (Before Moving To Main Island Creek)

JOHNSE

ELECTION DAY FIGHT

CAP

BATTLE OF GRAPEVINE CREEK

PIKE COUNTY, KY

VALENTINE "WALL" HATFIELD

ELIAS

"BAD" 'LIAS

ASA HARMON McCOY

TUG RIVER

Map Is Not To Exact Scale

OHIO

Ironton

Ashland
Catlettsburg
Huntington

KENTUCKY

Big Sandy

Blaine

Louisa

Tug Fork

WEST VIRGINIA

Paint

Pigeon

Beckley

Paintsville

Johns

Williamson

Prestonburg

Levisa Fork

Welch

Elkhorn

Pikeville

Knox

Dry Fork

Shelby

Elkhorn

Dismal

Bluefield

Elkhorn City

Russell Fork

McClure

Pound

Pine Mountain

Cranes Nest

Wise

VIRGINIA

Tazewell

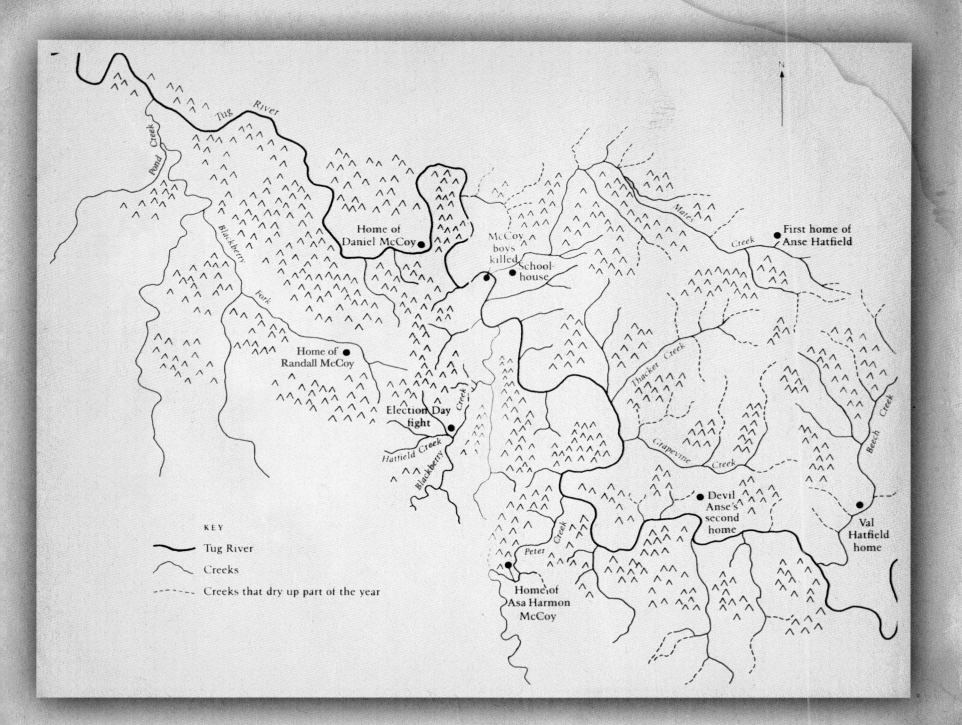

Home of
Daniel McCoy

McCoy
boys
killed

School-
house

First home of
Anse Hatfield

Mates

Creek

Home of
Randall McCoy

Thacker Creek

Election Day
fight

Creek

Hatfield Creek

Blackberry

Grapevine

Creek

Beech Creek

Devil
Anse's
second
home

Val
Hatfield
home

Peter

Creek

KEY

Tug River

Creeks

Creeks that dry up part of the year

Home of
Asa Harmon
McCoy

Tug River

Blackberry

Fork

Pond Creek

N

PHOTO CREDITS